Subpress 2006

IN CAPTIVITY

Acknowledgments:
Poems from this book have appeared in the following journals: *Artkrush.com, The Chicago Review, Conjunctions, The Gig, The Poetry Project Newsletter,* and *The Poker.* "Defending Oneself" was published as a chapbook online by Beard of Bees Press (www.beardofbees.com). Many grateful thanks to the editors of those publications.

I am indebted to Donna Stonecipher for her generous readings. I also wish to thank the following people for their encouragement and inspiration: Meghan Guthrie, Ann Lauterbach, Maria Fahey, Heather Ramsdell, Beth Anderson, and Eric Elshtain. As always, my affectionate thanks to my family.

Author photo: Cyrus Marshall
Book design: Anna Moschovakis

Cover image: *The Hunt of the Unicorn: The Maiden's Companion Signals to the Hunters* (detail). The Metropolitan Museum of Art, Gift of John D. Rockefeller Jr., 1938. (38.51.2) Photograph

In Captivity

ISBN-13: 978-1-930068-32-2
ISBN-10: 1-930068-32-8
Library of Congress Control Number: 2006933130

IN CAPTIVITY

POEMS BY

CAMILLE GUTHRIE

for Duncan

&

for Karen

Surely infiniteness is the most evident thing in the world

—George Oppen

TABLE OF CONTENTS

IN CAPTIVITY

The Start of the Hunt

I

How can empty space be stirred?
How to be truthful to one's words
Or a city person's longing for the country
Maybe a mistake of subject

Nevertheless, like a blank piece of paper
I drifted along past buildings
Straight or curved lines receding
Past unreadable stone steel and glass objects

Edges vibrating in the air, then vanishing at a touch
Withdrawing into cloudy heights
I walked up aimless blocks each day
Discord knocking about in my head

Sick with fear that had no form
Captured by my debt to pay
Wanting to make something of myself
Wanting knowledge & intimacy

Those actual facts
But even colors deceive continually
In a land of pictorial symbols
So I took directions from the lookout

His knees swallowed up by scenery
Attentive ripeness!
I am learning to see

2

What to bring on a Hunt:

A sense of boredom or awe, a need for lost rituals *&* early abundance,
a desire to miss nothing *&* a flashlight because it's early spring
that juxtaposition of the seen and unseen—if I say
'daffodil,' everyone thinks of a different radiant

In the deli you, the lookout,
observe the labels: 'BLUE CORNFLOWER
Clears Sight With Extra Snake Repellant'

A man in a white linen suit
with a crane's head for a hat
buys the news and a green carnation

The long-hour woman laughs
and wraps green onions in tissue paper,
'Be careful. This is very heavy'

A row of water bottles pulls me in
I step from that riverbed
I intend to make use of my time

3

No protection from the number
of individuals in the counterfeit city
its gewgaws and things to do
or from any marplot whose ruinous intent
ranges up the avenues

I walk past the illustrated hotel
The Hectic, the place of all my fears,
this is the starting point because I look for danger
everywhere putting out feelers

A panic spring, in alarm
not to be caught looking
having little choice but to see these extremities
having an interior I didn't know I had

Is this false world transitory?
But I know better
I'm taking action against fear
since I've come down with it

4

The hunters roam with their dogs
and hawkers too, mechanicals intent
in expensive striped suits
sure of their rightful possessions & desired effects
inscribing their accumulated landscape

Scent hounds slip from the shore:
Rashness, Desire, Anxiety, Fear & Grief
could ambush us you know
their snouts disappear into wild grasses

And beggars are fast about
rushing on trains or sleeping under benches
At any moment
the sound of all animals shouts out

Cacophony rings like unstoppable capital
its edges echo into the trees
Such riches there
to rot have run

5
The New York Public Library:

In the balmy enormity of the reading room
the ceiling a false sky unchanging blue
pink lit clouds roll above silent readers
I settle down and have a poet:
'An emphasis falls on reality'
(that's Barbara Guest)

And more distractions:
a lock of Mary Shelley's light hair,
Woolf's walking stick, susceptibility
caught in V.N.'s butterfly net,
sketched with Thoreau's pencil—
I guess I should get back to work

But it's noontime outside
clouds pace above the symmetry of industry
Trees in the park outline the wind
elm, linden, walnut, aspen, plum, ash, birch, palm, and oak
gradually shredding a motorcycle cover

So scrupulous, the density of things
keeps receding so far
I have to sidestep
the chemical gutter stream

6

Professionals in brown and orange uniforms nod
all manners of men, working & wandering
I'm with you

Who enter a room in suspension:
a Spider fills the dark circumference
protecting a damaged leg, scale is swollen
Residue of memory gnaws at a tapestry
one leg hooks out   Malevolence
we crawl under its fully black belly
You like to be threatened and look pleased

We see hanged faces and ravaged dolls
made up smudged concealed figurines
gravid ugly wasteland beauty
static women turning the same pages over & over

I prefer the blond ponytail in tablecloth skirt
waiting on the grey highway under a storm
her humble suitcase patient as a pet

Or gilt paint on small leaves
Gods with a lighter or a darker green heaven
Demons with a darker or lighter violet underworld
News prints fate maps blue prints
of continual creation, his humane narratives
(Blake wrote backwards & worked all night)

Or we're medieval, overlooking the Hudson
You say they're made of wool, silk, and metallic thread
the gold ones indicate the angle of sun
They were found covering potatoes in a barn
their royal emblems cut out to protect them
from the Reign of Terror with a note:

‘Examine these old tapestries.
Respect them because they show no signs of royalty.
They contain stories.’

7

Unruly creatures appear outside in metallic outfits
wrapped around the block, waiting in line
to hear music, they're wearing animal masks:
goldfinch lion panther genet hyena
stag rabbit bittern dragonfly
& a frog in the violets

Arch-eyed in round-toed slippers
and feathered vests, sporting spears,
pleasing figures pressed against asphalt curbs
now strewn with field daisies
because of their insouciance

Little pictures, idylls
of blowzy currency and indifference
I can't keep from looking
like blue and yellow making green
like constellations spinning in any direction
at any speed

Their raven snatches a shiny fleck
and makes off
I'm torn in two

8

Captured I stare at the green pool
on the gummy station floor
reflecting an escaped rat
until a pair of round lights
turns the corner, sound not arriving yet
and wait for the right letter

The cars next to us meet our speed
Faces drift into a lower cave
a stranger stares back at me and slips downward
shadows flashing linear pylons

A girl pins her boy to the door
'Darwin carried *Paradise Lost* in his pocket'
What happens if I expand while I'm reading
and can't fit in the car, elbows grazing the tunnels?

The dream girl ascends
from the subway having a fit so pregnable
those who wait are open-mouthed
wincing from the tyranny of the beautiful
and irreplaceable
                                        She leaps
yellow white red blue squares

Dew-fed and in a half dream another one
Wears a stolen broad-leaved pink on her jacket
Just corner her *&* make her give it back!

Bluebell lunaria wallflower
Cheap choice brave *&* new:
'Can I exchange it for another color?'
'Yes, they have all the best colors'

They step off into a taxi
to be encased like beetles
shiny alien untouchable, of definite value
'Beauty spent like Nature's coin'

9

A tree erupts from the sidewalk
A metal sign indents its arcature
The dogs all scatter receding into the woods
Drawn after better distractions

Rivers cast up many forms
To enter into the chaos of real things
But there's a penalty to beauty
And to know the word for a thing

Fix here you expectant spheres
And water towers over the city
Provable under the sun
I have been out

At the Fountain

When I first saw you
Pearled primed bearded beading
Gilt glossed arriving phantom
Creature kneels to drink

When I first saw you
Falling in the city, slipped between two rivers
I set aside my proclivity for loneliness
Set my heart on that springhead

I pass you a frond of my very wish
My genius for coming apart at the seams,
Changes of mood, statements of grief, wide-ranging ardor
If you talk to me, I change color

> Look me full in the face
> Give yourself to clarity
> Blue-green iridesce this way
> Your sound-and-light show

Overlooking my exaggerations,
The causes which lead you to become erect
And consequent changes of structure:
Increased size, absence of a tail, defenseless condition
Our various points of resemblance are luminous

Outside the arboreal library
Scrubby with reader's fatigue
I occupy my plans with the most important of all relations
'The lineaments of desire'
You took no notice

Raptly assembled piecework
Spikelet of laziness and love
Rapid increase! To have
The leafy facts of your unknown worlds
Which is what colors mean and natural light

Align our points of correspondence
The blue striped shirt, bone horns, sooty nose
And crush the ungetatable
Any reason for this endeavor seems true

You vary most Saturday afternoons
Ferns in the hair
Pulling off your Ovid t-shirt
Falling backwards into the bushes

I'm drawn in
By seemingly random behavior
'Whoso list to hunt'
How you like me now?

    Action of hand gestures
    Action of a bird landing
    Action of light on a hat

The amplification of small errors
Pinches the sore spot: clarity
Phantom limb pain and cases of difficulty
Knock the softling from its chair
Retracting one by one cobweb promises

I lay down in your night soil
Your leaf litter and bone meal
Your superphosphates
It was your bright idea

My insights into the absence of realism
Get me nowhere and show signs of distraction
I had a problem distinguishing the artificial lawns
The why stuck like sequins about your face
Just forget it!

The lower stages of your unconcern stun me
Detachment rips the only array I had
Cast in a frenzied outburst of my position
In the animal series:
Unmanned, unslaked, collapsible

Look, you suffer from overproduction
You're hand-made and overpriced
A.E. could mean many things
'Which one's to be master is all'

    Alas why do I love?
    So my eye is enthralled to your shape

Early spring crossed the stream in rubber boots
I rolled up the tapestry & tucked it under my head

Ground cherry & pseudo-narcissus
Landscape waves in and out
Headlong date palms display ciphers
In silver yarn tied with a bow

Hectic beauty prism saturation
Horizon light streak, risked enthusiasm
See here my heart, fringed facts
The surface so round, rare, a radiant thing
The fierceness of the specific
In slow motion capture

Drawn to these differences and origins
It's clear you have the cruelty to be interesting

Clatter of details asks all attention
It's easy to look at dark green edged with yellow
Articulated leaves, fragrant lit oval
The whole's the hard part

A bark, night-silvered
I fall victim to the symmetry of scenes
Look for you in the break in the trees

My Boyfriend

His Exterior

toes like blue glass marbles
nails like wax shavings
feet like those of an elephant
heels like narrow escapes
soles like yellow sponges expanding in water
legs like longitude and latitude
knees like neon headlights
thighs like open desert in a movie
hips like a leaping horse
a belly button like a luminescent watch
pubic hair like frontier instances
a penis like overnight mail
balls large as a boar-hound's
seminal vesicles like tulip bulbs in a paper bag
testicle muscles like rising chords
an asshole like an undiscovered planet
buttocks like a fleet antelope's
a sacrum like plein air painting
a back like a chalked sidewalk
a spinal column like a suspension bridge
ribs like a bookcase
a sternum like gum
shoulder blades like kitchen tables
a chest like a stuffed animal
pectorals like floating bars of soap
shoulders like observed facts
arms like lassos
fingers like sparklers
wrist bones like a shipyard
elbows like antidotes

hands like passports
an Adam's apple like a great circle course
a beard like Whitman's
a chin like a lichen-splotched rock
ears like a full bathtub
a nose like a birdcage
nostrils like subway tunnels
eyebrows like a captive audience
a birthmark like a stop sign
eyelids like a partial eclipse
eyes like effervescence
optical nerves like an orchid
a forehead like a window display
temples like singing crickets
cheeks like party invitations
jaws like handcuffs
teeth like sweet tea
a tongue like watercolors
a mouth like a silk lampshade
a face like a moving picture
a head like a jar of pennies
a skull like a geode
skin with a black line running down it
epidermis like a wool sweater
whiskers like a street sweeper
and hair like a cloudy day.

His Interior

cerebellum like a coffee grinder
cerebral lobes like a house on fire
cranial membranes like a construction-paper diorama
optical nerves like a developing Polaroid
cerebral fornix like colonial maps
pineal gland like a giant pinecone
circulatory system like cello strings
eardrums like a still life with oranges
forehead like television
backbone like a fiddlehead fern
nerve channels like transatlantic cables
uvula like a propeller
palate like a telegram
saliva like a rotating sprinkler
tonsils like action figures
stomach like professional wrestling
trachea like pirate radio
throat like a bold headline
lungs like plastic bags caught in a tree
heart like a supernova
pulmonary membranes like dirigibles
arteries like rush hour
diaphragm like the sound barrier
liver like a public trial
veins like Japanese characters
spleen like a rogue
bowels like surrealism
guts like an inheritance
small intestine like fake pearls
large intestine like stolen currency
colon like reliable data
rectum like a fade-out
kidneys like a barrier reef

loins like a mowed lawn
renal veins like gossip
sperm glands like lava beds
prostate like a fissure vent
bladder like a fish bowl
abdomen like a leather suitcase
muscles like an assembly line
tendons like pickpockets
ligaments like safety pins
bones like bones
marrow like realism
cartilage like strips of kelp
lymph glands like sentimentality
urine like sugar water
blood like melted crayons
and sperm like flies in amber.

How He Acts

If he laughs, it's spontaneous combustion
If he mutters, it's a retreating glacier
If he pouts, he sharpens his horn on stones
If he jumps up and down, it's hard to look away
If he scratches himself, it's with an aspen branch
If he gets angry, he fights with tooth, horn, and heel
If he spits, he fights his own kind
If he blows his nose, it starts a riot
If he sweats, it's monsoons
If he coughs, it unlocks doors in the next room
If he argues, it's over lost rituals
If he sighs, it ruffles goldfinch feathers
If he whistles, it's overheard miles away
If he snores, it's over nostalgic reveries
If he scowls, spears launch from his eyes
If he snorts, it's over gilt lion-head spouts
If he shits, it's historical documents
If he belches, it's a diary
If he vomits, there's finger-pointing all around
If he walks, it's Chaplin
If he writes, it's manifestos
If he goes shopping, it's for lentils and peas
If he dances, it's the Rites of Spring
If he swears, he's a ryght cruell beast
If he drives, it's among the Mountains of the Moon
If he bathes, it's in deceptive surfaces
If he dresses, it's a white linen suit
If he wonders, it's if his own reflection
If he's jealous, it's of birthday parties
If he lies, it's about mathematical errors
If he spends money, it's on magic lanterns
If he goes to the movies, it's *Vertigo*
If he listens to music, it's the sound of running water

If he falls, it's down a slope of turf into the bushes
If he recites, it's from the Beast Epic of Alexandria
If he is seduced, it's a river of electricity
If he is curious, he attempts to draw
If he calls, it's about weather patterns
If he sings, it's 'Tyger, Tyger'
and if he escapes, he's swift of foot.

A Memorable Fancy

1

There you were, listening to headphones
in straw hat, in verdure, gesturing for effect
clad in sandals & white t-shirt,
engaged in concentrated occupations
like looseleafery or exhaustive particulars

Wanting buoyancy and portable escapism
you crowded the moisture-loving space
with plants bought on the street
liking anything tangible and light green
in your enthusiasm for encouraging actual facts

You fancied allegory of all sorts
driving upstate, an original experience between us
playing the familiar:
'Let me take you to the movies
Can I make your garden grow?'

Sitting in the dark to watch slow-motion silver faces
Black gauze scarf lit against the impeccable white coat
'You took no notice'
Close-up everything

Everything taking part
& nothing lacking

2

I am thinking of
explicit sun you sit
under a blue plum tree, reading
as you are likely to do, crushed moss
underneath, aloof you pick
nettles from ripped jeans, tuck
a teasing foot under
thoughts press against thoughts
drawing narcissi, unmistakable
the toothing of their leaves
ferns turn over the sound of water
eyelash inky smudge
You missed a spot

There

My head held against your chest
unhurried night leaves its lair
arms round limitless present and we
listen to old records:
                                        'I'll   wait

till   your   love   comes   down'

Fix here

3

The bare fact

'IN MY LIFE I LOVE YOU MORE'

painted in thick white letters
up the block on my street
these costly details
laden mind
your color is almost
never seen as it really is

I lie in my bed four flights up
thinking we're not the heron who
flies above clouds to avoid tempests
but the common sparrow inquisitive
shadows jump fire escape rungs

From where I'm watching half-asleep
suffering from the image of you underwater
climbing out shooklight particles
Unbound abundance
yet small of mold

Who can restrain you? Reveal
yourself, I can't do everything

My Informants

Insist to have seen his bones.
Even Aristotle believed
in him, in two kinds.

Caesar on horseback
saw him hide in a forest.
I hear he appeared

To the mother of Confucius
with a tablet of jade
in his mouth. Many

Caravan journeys deep,
my informants send me to
the tax-gatherers of Persia.

Suffering from this so-called
holy disease, I taste his bitter flesh
a delicacy in these parts

And recall his solitude and habit of fighting.
Wearing a single spike on my forehead
attached to a flat leather helmet

Hopefully, I wait under the trees
receptive and lonely with little
defense against his poison.

The Elder Pliny says he
cannot be taken alive,
he smells like a virgin,

If crushed in wine, he banishes sadness,
bad dreams, evil thoughts. I took a dose
of four grains to half a scruple,

Sometimes a whole scruple and more.
Leading a violent career in the woods
he lives mainly on sugarcane,

My informants,
like a three-legged ass,
vaguely like antelopes.

In this realm ravaged by troubles,
of stolen lands, show trials, war,
disease, & intrigue, I'm powerless

But not useless like other things.
He might escape notice of those
who have already been there

If only everything would appear
as it truly is: Infinite.
As it is, I'm lost in the Contraries.

The Hunters

A green hunter a cloudy hunter a flashing hunter
A nightingale hunter a fixed hunter an infinite hunter
A midnight hunter an ocean hunter a thing hunter
A yes hunter a bodiless hunter a genius hunter

A deep hunter a collapsed hunter a starry hunter
A half-thought of hunter a velocity hunter a fate hunter
A truth hunter an image hunter a master hunter
A philosopher hunter a blue-red hunter an emerging hunter

A wished-for hunter a serpent hunter a supernatural hunter
A difference hunter a tragedy hunter a floating hunter
A misery hunter a just hunter a wild hunter
A calamity hunter a whole hunter a sense hunter

A quiet hunter an empty hunter a bubbling hunter
A naked hunter a humanity hunter a postponed hunter
A brilliant hunter a flecked hunter a canceled hunter
A chilled hunter a hotel hunter a measuring hunter

A daffodil hunter a dwarfed hunter a mother hunter
A polar hunter an azalea hunter a beaded hunter
A tipping hunter a scratching hunter an ether hunter
A fresh hunter a flying hunter a relentlessly hunter

A moony hunter a purifying hunter a tin hunter
A sharp hunter a dewy hunter a farewell hunter
A dissolving hunter a contained hunter a pacific hunter
A prescient hunter a blaze hunter an innocence hunter

A destiny hunter a leafless hunter an argument hunter
A purple-plated hunter a grassy hunter a peaches hunter
A mask hunter a sublime hunter a fang hunter
A brush-strokes hunter a drama hunter a flippant hunter

A moment hunter a flowery hunter a water hunter
A spirit hunter a malice hunter a curious hunter
A merely hunter an expensive hunter an enfolded hunter
A honey hunter a too hunter a tomorrow hunter

An object hunter an imperfect hunter an absence hunter
A paradise hunter a never-failing hunter a book hunter
A false hunter a brute-like hunter a theme hunter
A chance hunter a luminous hunter a matter hunter

My Psychomachia

My psychomachia, a close friend, moves in a seesaw motion, a symmetry of action
Occupied with the endless task of engraving things in the mind
Into little islands of desire, a kind of permanence: the magic of names.
These attempts, anguished creatures, do not arrive resounding train-like
At a green destination; nevertheless, made out of hopefulness my words
In their best order wish to enter into the chaos of real things.

Are words but a hunt for the shadows of things?
Do I suit the action to the word, the word to the action?
I try. Almost any image, idea, or object, I fit into an arrangement of words
For this machine and its glistening coils, which possesses my mind
Unrelentingly. I only think I have control. Well, it's a sort of pain I like
Which I can explain as a super-abstract withdrawal into a universe of names

Since it's so much easier to manipulate names:
Candor, childhood, CA, Coleridge—much better than the real things
That escape me: camels, clover, cuckoos, coal, coconuts. Do you like
Allegory? No? Look, what appears to be rigidity in action
May actually result in the product of an iridescent mind
Like Cézanne's, for example. This is when I fear the enchanting effect of my words

On others! Emerson too said: words are a kind of action, actions words.
Even when describing you in classic formulas or pastoral names,
Like 'Love's dart that wounds but does not kill,' the mechanical mind
Selects terms to express its ambivalence about beloved things.
I wish I were more like Rilke, who in his youth wrote: 'I am taking action
Against fear,' or like Zola, who said, 'I always bite off more than I can chew like

When I attack a subject I really like
I try to force a whole illuminated world into words;
Hence my torments, in my ambition for drama shifting into action,

For immortal moments and names.'
I too long for this exacting world built from the actualities of things
Dusted off and slipped into the reader's restless mind.

A high degree of intensity can lurk in the back of one's mind
That must be out. When I realized I had this problem, more or less like
Others, I pinned above my desk: 'The poet flees from the macrocosm of things
To the microcosm of words.' To the microcosm of words.
And: 'He loves the fatal fictions, cloudy figures, and shadowy names
For their own sake, dazed by the unruly content of his dreams in action.'

I don't mind it at all. It becomes a familiar sort of engaging action
Like favorite lines one says over and over to oneself: tender names.
He who knows the word for a thing I know masters the thing.

A Complaint

My decisions finally arrive at your green destination
Where flat coursing blue presses against repetitious trees.
I see you crammed the joint with symbolic flowers
All referring to your better qualities. (Purity? Clarity? Huh.)

Leaves ruff yellow and cherries wink light.
However, that is not one of those
And these roses are not wild. The fence flies
Up, a hand falls on my neck: a setup.

By the time you pull in, sovereign of my woods
And twice the height of a fruit-bearing bush,
I'm already taken in by your round grey eye. Stop
Tying your initials to branches with silk cords—
You can't defy gravity or any force older than you.

Well, we all succumb to Mary and get incarnate
Especially when someone's wearing that old blue chaplet
Seeming to smile. Take me alive to the palace
Of the king, whatever that means.

Headlong a swift hand
was needed to
unfasten the buttons of
your pea coat.

In single combat
may as well say uncle
and pay the penalty of beauty.
Your collar's twisted—
here I'll fix it.

Later, girls tie themselves to trees to play Lure-the-Beast.
A pretty boy can do it in a dress. They all reach
Forth to grab the horn, singing. But why
Conduct private rituals in public, and so formally?

Your sidekick appears in red cap with tinsel horn.
His dog lifts a rascal tail. Now no one
Can take a nap on our street. Here comes
Your maid cinching her dress inflected with color
To make her seem real. Her pony
Tail dangles like a threat.

In her lap or at her breast
I'm inclined to take
advantage of the lake to
bite the rough end off.

Dogs land on my back
press my face against
cement. Mice chew
at my ankles.

No wonder I look darkly on the cheat
As you march into the lake with dandelion garlands.
I never wanted to be your handmaiden
Pencil driving in a rose-entwined enclosure.

Put away the 15th century encyclopedia now,
Reality-testing is what we're up to.
How does matter behave under tremendous pressure?
I almost wrote pleasure.

Defending Oneself

With a lonely girl's lust
For allegorical violets, for violent underbrush
Symbolic leaflet and narrative bractlet
I fell hard for the actual facts

With a girl's deliria
For the interpretation of dreams
For inflorescence and shaping fantasies
Sleep finally brought my night thoughts

Fresh happiness
May much gelato melt on your face
May you be indifferent to street humidity
And your comets arrive on time

Come, when soaked with sweat or dew
You send up bubbles into the half-distance
When singed, you give off a sweet odor
Hey, shed irony! I'm not so ugly

If you will only try a summer in pastoral poverty
Looting and roaming at will
We'll perform classical rituals of battle and mating
Watch the satellite flicker in the evenings

June urgently agrees with July I'm ready
For youknowwhat don't change your mind
Let's exchange numbers and forked lightning
Let's do what's sure as fate now

Knocked up on demented love
Fucked up on powdered swallow's heart
Laced with a scruple of heron's liver
That was merely the beginning

Dispatched down perplexed paths
Why the hand-cuffs? he asks
Since I can read sun-spots I knew
He grew Love-in-a-mist with another

The finest I could've afforded
I sent him ten pairs of antique Levi's
Ass soft as a rabbit napping on moss
I'll overnight twelve more Tuesday

Forget it all, Leaf Litter
Your letters were shredded in the Reign of Terror
Then used to cover potatoes from frost
It was a fairy vision

True and False Heart
She'll do it you can count on it
She'll chop off their candied heads
And pretend not to like the sound effects

I'll still speak to her reddening while we talk
But only in answering couplets
She—celebrated oil of vermin
Me—genuine dust of scorpion

Just stop speaking to me, Petticoat
Better not invite my legendary wrath
A rumor spread by the Crusades
I gave away my copy of your first book

Busy with the history of your problems
Your fretful singing swept through an abandoned lot
Throw it in the East River, dear
And never look back

That's it for our time-scarred friendship
I must be viewless in a no-place place
Scratching at my sticky wounds
Half-crustacean half-alicorn half-orangutan

All brightness spent like play money
And fistfuls of frozen words that won't crack
Even if you jump up *&* down on them
And you didn't call me even when I was sick

Don't turn to me as a friend two months late
All innocent like a new spatula
I expect you for dinner promptly at eight
One sip of this and you're finished

Why be so awful to yourself?
I'm not neglecting your messages
At least stop sulking & kicking up dust
Like an ant swallowing aspirin

What more can I offer you, Pudding Mouth?
Not gorgeous no-fault loans
No more weekends on rented islands
No crazed pleasure gripping protected wetlands

You astonish me
Like a trapdoor in the superhighway
G'head, sink the convertible in the ocean
Just give me back my money

Those upperschool poets pelt us with dried mud
We duck and run for cover
Any fruit aisle at the bodega will do
Or just move to a cheaper borough

Errant intruders were ripped to pieces
Then, wounds, well-aimed, were self-inflicted
As they drifted to the infamous islands
Wordless & Formless & Artless

That unlucky filly, Small Talk
Fancies herself a bite of the sublime
Vulgar errors in form and content
We'll overlook no more than five

Don't look so stricken
She won't notice you in that ineffable jacket
She goes by as if stepping on knives
Doll-heart only goes for the real article

I know where you're hiding
You can't escape me now
I'll unravel every secret code
I have night vision goggles

I can't think of you that fondly
When much precious juice was pressed
For the hung-over city
But that's a pregnant question

Now what has possessed you?
You drag me off to see the troll-like art
Of some leading man of the young foresters
Whose skull was split by snapdragons

The choice was made
The bumpkin sucked up, a sign of things to come
Now he's well-connected, wholesale
In royal ballet ecstasy circles

Like panthers in a parking garage
Consents & Disagreements did terror to each other
What do you want me to do about it?
I'm under the thumb of a tyrannical waiter

Seen kissing the worst ex-novelist downtown
And fifteen other egregious charges
You have my deepest sympathy
You could do better

He detected fear in my early work
'But this is what I see, this is what I see,' I repeated
Is it really his and not someone else's venom?
Who else would want to poison you

Hanging about shifting for invitations
Now your heart-sleeves amuse them all
Even their hounds are whipped into a frenzy
Hurry, they're starting the dying of the Republic

A nasty and persistent hobby
You foolishly believe is funny
You borrow a book without telling me
My only signed copy of *The Eclogues*

Bored too long with apologies
I want my copy of *Comus* back
Which you fake is your own first edition
Imposter! Why not move back to Boston

I see you at a singing match to exchange insults
Stop writing like you're minting green stuff
And fumbling with high-toned language
Like the doleful penis of a Formalist gentleman

The time for flayed rhymes has ended
You'll succeed in your objective to wreck my confidence
Unless crushed, Pot Licker
First and completely by me and my band

Into the dumpster down the dead end
Vapid verses & so-called knowing
Chasing barren ideas in a gritty wind
Into the gutter into the sidewalk trash can

In the Battle of the Books they will surely lose
Fatal as they are fee-faw-fo-fum
Their words will fade from the universe
No one will daydream of them

Yell yourself sick to death
Words like yours inspire no fear
You're jealous, your poems are bereft
Yet I drink at the fountain

It's not what you expected
I only wanted the actual facts
You can't touch my mind
With all your false charms

You say I'm too sensitive
You say 'That's so over' So what
It's not the what it's the how
I don't want your truthless love anymore

I know what you'll deserve in the afterlife
Surrounded by your moldering theories
I can predict this by my art
We who burn in a purer fire

The Contraries

I have a young sister of promise
Far beyond the city where I work
Her hair is brown, her eyes flower black
My letters are sent back to me

Dead set on a particular man
To fill her days with delight
The dress she wore was blue
On that day his suit radiated light

When he took his urgent will of her
The man his heart was lawless & maimed
He cut her down in the bramble street
For talking to him in public like that

You may go & you may leave
The enemy he lifts a hand against me
I've told you many times before
We're lost in the contraries

I have a young brother full of will
Far beyond the city where I walk
He's in pursuit of the actual facts
His mind it flies so eagerly

The hunters they ran him down
They fell on him in the dirty street
And smashed his head with a bat
For talking in public like that

They took his books & his bones
Raised a hand against his words
Worth more than a city
They took his bit of immortality

You may leave or you may go
So I told you times before
My enemy lays his hands on me
And we're lost in the contraries

One night as I was walking
Down a familiar street where I live
I stopped to sit under a smoke tree
Thinking this may bring you back to me

My thoughts of you come so eagerly
'So ho, boy, illo ho'
Just like so many times before
I am drawn by your sweetness alone

When we watched the black river
Cloud flying darkly above our city
I pulled a piece of paper from the sky
Now I'm taking action against fear

You may go & you may leave
When the enemy lays its hands on me
But today I'm lost in the contraries
Lost in the powerful contraries

In Captivity

I

Everyone hears the clamorous refrain
Drowned in his streaming passage
He is out of reach a world within
I'll listen to him again

He stepped out from a lava bed
To compose the engine of his ruin
He took the bait, wanting to be tested
By experience and fatal fictions

Fix here you overheated spheres
That wrestle the foot of time
Begin then the clashing burden
Of his restless song

2

They raised you up under the apple tree
Lifting a hand against your overcast wonder
They'll do you mischief in the shrubbery
And in the evergreens believe it

Your dad he lit you up and stepfathers
Chased you from farmland to suburb
Hunters, lumbermen, fishermen
Crushed you in their midst

Slurred small silent
Dropped out bruised bored
Lying on railroad tracks, fucking backward girls
But it's the wrong track and her dad found out

Boys in Captain America t-shirts
Pin you down, getting high in the woods,
Force you into a rusted trunk and nightly
Behead you behind the high school

Homeless bliss & weekend antics
Hurl you back into your first being
Studying the legends of errant genius
Their outsized madness is only half-false

Sleeping in a lawless placeless place
Under a bridge to dream up racking up
Misadventures 'and plenty of money
And sang to a small guitar'

But somebody jumps you behind the 7-Eleven
Or eviscerates you at a basement club
Where ambition is your only armor

Like a lion's head helmet waiting in a museum
                                        for you to pick it up

Captured, you put your hand
On the key to forget everything
A potion of planetary dust
I'll apply to your eye   I'll   apply
                                        to   your   eye

3

‘There was a young man in a dirty shirt
Who ran away to see the constellations of night,
But the satellites of the air filled him with despair,
And oppressed that young singer of the night.’

4

How to show the whole scene in flames
How to transform a mudslide into a man
How to split the night with lightning
How to make a cloud with people on it descend
        onto the stage from the sky

You come on stage wheelchair-bound bearded old man
Infirmities press against caves of the mind
Backlit figures put out a thousand lures
There came fame: the Withdrawing Hand

From grizzly loser bleary trespassing janitor
You wander everywhere, you are translated
With the power to cheat the eye with illusion
With your brutal words your tender chaos

Bleached face nails red eyes rimmed black
Erratic wreck clatter rip chords in a housedress
Persuasion & truth in mythy strokes
You knew how to build a rhyme & destroy it

Ultraviolet the crowd waits in suspension
A rout of monsters their heads like wild beasts
Wolf bear leopard tiger hog bearded goat
Making riotous & unruly noise

Boys cry out from cavernous bedrooms
Brokenheel girls offer up pearled wrists
For livid dark won't be present for long
'Suppression prepares for Overflow'

Your songs are sold down the stream
Emblems of the night's accidents
Repetition tells you there is some error
Did you take too much or too little?

Now increase the rate of radiance
This way your noise went

5

Here comes the fury
To cut your throat to cut
Your thin-spun life here
Comes your self-inflicted curse:

'May I never exist may I never
May my body face hands never exist may
My past my actions never exist
May my breath sounds words never exist'

Clamor marks the moment
Night-foundered-shotgun-TV-on
Copycats caught up in your dark spell
Taking action against fear

They leave notes tears trinkets
Pansies carnations freakt with jet
Rampion marigold daffadillies
And flag iris freakt with shadow

Girls hide make-believe artifacts under canopies
Boys tear down posters and unload pellet guns
Maddened by your music the captors
Dismember you *&* toss your head into the river

6

But O the change now you're on the other side
Round the vanishing point & never coming back
Overlapping sounds pass you by
You're intractable with no fixed address

Nature bolts beyond you
With more significant disasters to mind
Flooding the towns you played drowning their museums
The deep shuts over your head

Fill the air with dissonance
Send up electric currents
Fix here you blasted spheres
That wing the relentless foot of time

Captured by your debt to pay
You are the genius of this shore
And will be truthful to your words
To all who listen from here on

AUTHOR'S NOTE

This book is a loose response to the *Unicorn Tapestries* (1495–1505), which are kept in the Cloisters of the Metropolitan Museum of Art. There are a few echoes of Rilke's *The Notebooks of Malte Laurids Brigge* in "The Start of the Hunt." "My Boyfriend" is modeled after a list in Rabelais's *Gargantua and Pantagruel.* Brief lyrics from Led Zeppelin, Van Halen, and The Beatles appear in "A Memorable Fancy." "My Informants" uses language from Odell Shepard's *The Lore of the Unicorn*. "My Psychomachia" is indebted to Angus Fletcher's book *Allegory: The Theory of a Symbolic Mode*. The final poem engages with Milton's *Comus* and "Lycidas," with a bit of Edward Lear and of *A Midsummer Night's Dream*.

Camille Guthrie was born in Seattle and grew up in Pittsburgh. She attended Vassar College and Brown University, and then settled in New York City where she teaches literature and creative writing. Her first book, *The Master Thief*, was published by Subpress in 2000. She lives in Brooklyn with her husband and son.

BOOKS FROM SUBPRESS

Scott Bentley / *The Occasional Tables*
Daniel Bouchard / *Diminutive Revolutions*
Daniel Bouchard / *Some Mountains Removed*
Sherry Brennan / *Of Poems and Their Antecedents*
Catalina Cariaga / *Cultural Evidence*
Steve Carll & Bill Marsh / *Tao Drops, I Change*
Jordan Davis & Sarah Manguso (Eds.) / *Free Radicals: American Poets Before Their First Books*
Linh Dinh / *All Around What Empties Out*
kari edwards / *a day in the life of p.*
Joe Elliot / *Opposable Thumb*
Brett Evans / *After-School Session*
Robert Fitterman & Dirk Rowntree / *WAR, the musical*
Benjamin Friedlander / *The Missing Occasion of Saying Yes: Poems 1984–1994*
Camille Guthrie / *The Master Thief*
Roberto Harrison / *Os*
Jen Hofer / *Slide Rule*
Rob Holloway / *Permit*
Jeff Hull / *Spoor*
Denizé Lauture / *The Black Warrior and Other Poems*
Steve Malmude / *The Bundle: Selected Poems*
John McNally / *Exes for Eyes*
Hoa Nguyen / *Your Ancient See Through*
Deborah Richards / *Last One Out*
Prageeta Sharma / *Bliss to Fill*
Caroline Sinavaiana-Gabbard / *Alchemies of Distance (with Tinfish)*
James Thomas Stevens & Caroline Sinavaiana / *Mohawk/Samoa: Transmigrations*
Edwin Torres / *Fractured Humorous*
John Wilkinson / *Oort's Cloud: Earlier Poems (with Barque)*